Self-Care

for Foster and Adoptive Families

What Others are Saying

♥♥♥♥♥♥♥♥♥♥♥♥♥♥♥♥♥♥♥♥♥♥♥♥♥♥♥♥♥♥

"Self-Care for Foster and Adoptive Families", by Sharla Kostelyk, is a must read for anyone thinking of fostering or adopting, and also for those who are well into their journeys of fostering and/or adoption. As a relatively new foster and adoptive parent, I laughed and cried my way through this helpful guide as I recognized Sharla's struggles as my own, realized that I am not alone, and found solutions to help me through the difficult days. With her non-judgement knowledge and wit, Ms. Kostelyk gives realistic advice for fostering and adoptive families. Self care is a critical part of preparing and succeeding at the foster and adoption ride of your life!"

– Michelle, foster and adoptive mom

"Kostelyk's book is a finger firmly on the pulse of adoption's specific challenges. This is an important and overdue survive and thrive manual born out of Sharla's own experiences, trials, errors and successes. I applaud adoptive parents for there is nothing more important than providing a safe and loving home for a child. This book is your tool to make your lives easier and ensure your family's success and happiness."

–Cathy Klapstein, Foster Care Agency Employee

"I have read numerous articles on how to prepare for the day when our child finally comes home. Sharla has exceeded them by far! Her attention to the big and little details in preparing for the arrival of the child, and then surviving the actual event is so incredibly practical, convicting and encouraging all at the same time. The tips in this book are so terribly necessary to making a new family's first few months together be as successful as possible. I would love to see this e-book be required reading of every waiting adoptive or foster parent."

–Denise Naus, mother of 3 – one by birth, one adopted at birth, and waiting to bring home one more miracle

"I had the opportunity to read Sharla's book while in the trenches of being a newbie adoptive mom. It was a real encouragement to me to learn what I was doing right and what I could do differently to enable me to still feel like me and not feel like I was drowning in mothering three very needy little girls. I highly recommend that every newly adoptive parent take the time to read this book. You owe it to yourself!"

–Deborah, adoptive mom

❤❤ Table of Content ❤❤

♥♥ Introduction ♥♥

We have all heard the parenting analogy of having to put on our own oxygen mask before putting the masks on our children. The thinking behind this is of course that we must put our mask on first to make sure we are conscious to put the masks on them. As caregivers, we must take care of ourselves so that we are able to give full and proper care to our children. However, actually putting this into practice in our everyday lives is difficult for most parents and it can seem nearly impossible for foster and adoptive parents.

Self-care is even more important for foster and adoptive parents than it is for other parents because foster and adopted children require more from their caregivers and the stakes are much higher.

Foster parents are in very high demand. There are not enough foster homes in this country to meet the growing number of children entering into foster care. There are even fewer foster parents who are qualified to meet the needs of the growing number of children entering the child welfare system requiring specialized care. This results in greater demands being put on existing foster families, which often results in foster parent burnout. With such overwhelming demands being put onto foster parents, how do they make time for self-care?

Adoption disruption rates are also on the rise. Adoption disruption occurs when an adoptive family is unable to continue to care for their adopted child and that child is placed into foster care or another adoptive home. Though a failed adoption is obviously a worst case scenario for a child who has already lost his or her birth family, it is also devastating for the adoptive family. It is not something that any family resorts to lightly and the judgment and guilt the family experiences during and after the failed adoption is both heartbreaking and debilitating.

Not all adoption disruption and foster care burnout can be prevented, but by laying and maintaining a solid foundation of self-care and making it non-negotiable in your household, you can help protect yourself and your family from some of the pitfalls that may otherwise await you. Consider self-care the best shield of protection your family can have.

I am not an expert in self-care. After our two sons were born, we were foster parents for eight years. We went on to adopt three of our foster children and then adopted two children internationally. In the course of what would be eleven years between when we began the journey to expand our family and when we brought our last two children home, I made a lot of mistakes when it came to self-care. Later, when I began my work as an adoption advocate, I heard first-hand countless stories from others who were suffering because of what boiled down to a lack of self-care.

It is my hope that these suggestions help others who are on the journey to adoption, have already adopted, or are fostering. I still am better at talking the talk than walking the walk, so writing this has also been a good reminder to myself! Self-care is something that is a conscious decision and something that doesn't come naturally for me, so I hope that you will join me on the journey and we can find our way together.

❤❤ Why Self-Care? ❤❤

Self-care is a skill. It is like most other skills in that you get better at it the more you learn about it and the more you practice it. You cannot be there for your family and friends if you have not taken care of yourself first. Burnout occurs with stress. Poor stress management leads to physical and emotional exhaustion. Caregivers are at higher risk of depression, divorce, addictions, significant health problems, and earlier death. If these reasons are not important enough for you to begin to put effort in to managing your own self-care, consider the example you are setting for your children.

Modeling self-care for your children teaches them self-regulation, enabling them to make better decisions. This translates into their thinking, emotions, and behavior. If you have been successful in calmly expressing your feelings, they will be able to articulate their own emotions and with your help, find an outlet for expressing those emotions. Children do not learn stress management techniques unless they are taught them and see them put into practice. If children see their parent stuffing their feelings inside, playing the martyr, overextending themselves, and burning out, those are likely patterns they will follow later in life as well.

By modeling to your child that when you have a need such as hunger or thirst, you satisfy that need, you are teaching your child to listen to their own bodies, decreasing their risk of sexual abuse and eating disorders.

By creating a system in which your children learn that your marriage, your beliefs, your mental, spiritual and physical health, and your friendships are a priority, you are increasing the odds that your child will place a high priority on these things as well when they reach adulthood themselves.

In creating for yourself a strong support network, you are

gifting your child with more people in their life to love them, build into them, and influence them.

The biggest reason of all to practice self-care is to live the best life you can live. You deserve it and your family deserves it too.

Preparations

The foundations of self-care can actually begin long before a family adopts or begins fostering. By preparing yourselves and those around you for what is to come, you will be better equipped when it finally happens.

If your child is already at home and you did not take these steps ahead of time, do not panic! Skim this section to determine if there are steps here that you can implement now and prepare for in the future should you decide to add to your family.

Education

The first step in preparation is education. Before embarking on the fostering or adoption journey, read as much as possible about what to expect. Depending on your circumstances, this may include arming yourself with knowledge about attachment, the stages of grief, fostering, adoption, the effects of malnutrition on the developing brain, or various types of special needs such as Fetal Alcohol Spectrum Disorder (FASD) and Sensory Processing Disorder (SPD).

Many adopted children are impacted by the effects of trauma on their early brain development whether prenatally or postnatally. I highly recommend that you read the book The Connected Child by Dr. Karyn Purvis. You can find other resources for attachment and trauma at Empowered to Connect.

Knowledge really is power. While you still have the time, during your wait for a foster or adoption placement, take advantage of seminars, conferences and webinars that will help equip you with tools that you can use down the road.

Another source of knowledge is other parents who are

at various stages of the process. Talking to them is very important as it will give you a more complete picture of what to expect. People who are still in the waiting stage of the adoption journey and have not yet brought home a child will be able to share with you the potential disappointments and heartbreaks that occur along the way and the emotional roller-coaster that is the road to adoption.

Those who have recently adopted or begun fostering may share that they feel overwhelmed. Those families who are further down the road may be able to give a more complete picture of the joys that fostering or adoption can bring, but also some of the difficulties they have encountered along the way. Veteran foster parents will be able to give you perspective on how they were able to cope when children they loved had to leave their homes and how they handled difficult placements.

As RAD (Reactive Attachment Disorder) is one of the most severe challenges associated with adoption, be sure to talk to parents that have walked that road as well. You may be inclined to believe that it could never happen to you (as we once naively thought) but in the world of adoption, it can happen to any family. Being prepared can help. Finding families with children affected by common diagnoses in the adoption world such as ADHD, SPD, RAD, and FASD can also help you down the road as they will be a good resource for you to turn to.

Relationships

If you are married, the time to strengthen your marriage is BEFORE you bring another child into your home. If there are areas of conflict in your relationship, they will only grow once adoption or fostering compounds the stresses in your home. Therefore, the best time to deal with those conflicts is right now. If your styles of communicating are unhealthy, seek the advice or services of a counselor and be sure to lay a solid foundation of healthy communication in your marriage. I have laid out further suggestions for this in the Marriage chapter.

Financial

Finances are something that most of us do not want to look at too closely. We would rather not know even though the not knowing can cause worry. Expending energy worrying about debt or upcoming bills is draining.

Most types of adoption cost a substantial amount of money, potentially stretching an already tight budget. In addition, there is the cost of raising an extra child or extra children, the cost of childcare or possibly the lost wages of one parent staying at home. This all causes a huge financial adjustment and needs to be planned for accordingly.

By sitting down ahead of time and budgeting monthly expenses, setting aside an emergency fund, and figuring out a strategy for paying the adoption costs, you will save yourself money and future stress. A resource that I recommend for this step is Dave Ramsey's book, _The Total Money Makeover_.

If you do not have enough money set aside to cover the cost of adoption without going further into debt, there are alternatives. Government adoption is free and in some provinces, there is even ongoing financial support until that child turns 18.

If government adoption does not seem right for your family, consider fundraising for all or a portion of your adoption costs. We were able to raise $6,200 for our adoption from Ethiopia by doing a clothing and bake sale and a garage sale. There are many more fundraising ideas. With a bit of work and creativity, some families have been able to cover their entire adoption expenses.

People often overlook the toll that financial stress takes.

Finances are the number one cause of divorce in North America and can lead to stress related illnesses. Financial stress is not something that should be ignored and it can be a major contributor to problems after an adoption takes place if people do not prepare themselves financially.

For foster parents, even though fostering provides a small additional income, finances are something that should be looked at and discussed before the fostering journey begins. If the fostering income is at least partially applied to debt or savings and there is a plan in place, there will most likely be more peace in the home. By having a plan for your spending, saving, and potential emergencies in place before you adopt or begin fostering, you will improve communication in your marriage, take the fear out of your financial needs, and feel more confident going into the process. You will also relieve the burden of stress that disorganized finances cause and get on the road toward a healthier financial future. The small income that fostering brings in cannot necessarily be counted on. Unforeseen circumstances such as a foster child leaving or you adopting your foster child mean that the fostering income is no longer there. If you budget in such a way that that income isn't counted on for regular household expenses and particularly if you saved much of that income, then those times do not become stressful.

Practical

Practical preparations before a new child enters your family ensure that you are able to spend the most time possible on attachment, family unity and adjusting once your child is home.

One practical suggestion is to de-clutter your house. You can contribute to preparing your finances and give yourself a deadline for the de-cluttering if you have a garage sale. It is a great excuse to sort through your cupboards, closets, garage, and storage rooms and purge your home of unwanted and unused items.

Preparation also includes tackling any projects around the house or yard that need to be done but seem to just stay in the back of your mind. Completing those projects will free your mind from nagging thoughts and free up your time when your child is home.

Another thing I suggest you do when preparing for a new child is to prepare meals. This can be done by making multiple months of freezer meals, meal planning, or by creating a plan for friends and family to sign up for bringing meals over to your house once you come home with your new child.

When we were adopting, I made freezer meals. I planned what to make, went shopping for the ingredients, had my mom and sister-in-law help chop vegetables and cook meat, and then two friends came to help me assemble the meals. In total, there were almost 80 meals made over two days. This lasted months after we brought our new children home and it took an enormous weight off of me in those early weeks of adjustment. If you decide to meal plan, then I suggest that you keep the recipes simple and do as much as you can ahead of time, including writing out at least six weeks' worth of meal plans with corresponding grocery lists.

Take this time of waiting to schedule and attend any appointments or meetings that you may have been putting off. Procrastination breeds its own stress. Go to the dentist, get your wisdom teeth pulled, meet with the accountant, make a legal will, make any phone calls you have been dreading, forgive the person you need to forgive, get those pants hemmed, take the used books to a consignment store, have a full medical exam done, apply for life insurance, take your vehicle in for a tune-up, take a deep breath and have the confrontation you have been avoiding, and check off any other tasks on your mental to-do list. This will free up head space and time. Whatever is left undone will expend emotional energy that could be better used elsewhere.

Another consideration in preparation is to get your body ready. Begin to eat healthier meals and exercise. Get adequate sleep each night. Your sleep pattern is likely to be interrupted once your child is home, regardless the age of the child you are fostering or adopting. Babies obviously wake up in the middle of the night, but older children sometimes have night terrors or have a hard time falling asleep in a new home. With internationally adopted children, there will be jet lag. If you are working on attachment, you may be co-sleeping with your child, so one way or another, there is bound to be less sleep in your future. Get some sleep while you can. If it is possible, take naps, even if it is just one afternoon a week. Prepare your body so that your immune system will be strong and your body will have reserves from which to draw when you need them.

Develop healthy habits now so that it will be easier to keep those habits going once your child is home. If you are not already taking proper care of yourself, it will be nearly impossible to do it once things turn upside down for a time in your life. Set up a solid foundation of self-care even before your child is home.

The last practical preparation that I recommend is harder than all the rest, but is one of the most important. Look at how you are currently spending your time and think realistically about how those things will fit into your new life of being an adoptive or foster parent. It is likely that when you see objectively how many hours are already spoken for, you will realize that there are some sacrifices that need to be made. Write down the areas that are your priorities. This will help you in making decisions about what things need to be cut out of your life for the season you are approaching. Most people do not do this step prior to bringing their child home. They wait until their child is home already and when they feel like they are drowning, they then try to make changes. THIS DOES NOT WORK.

If you wait until you are under stress to make these changes in your life, you are not likely to make good choices. You will also be overextended to the point where you will most likely not have time to sit back and look at your true priorities and make logical choices. The other risk of waiting until after your child is home to make these choices is that you may resent them for it. Clear space in your schedule NOW.

By educating yourself on what lies ahead, strengthening your marriage, becoming financially and physically fit, and making room in your life to prepare your home, meals, and schedule, you will set the stage for a healthy transition when the time comes for your child to come home.

❤❤ Support Network ❤❤

Creating a framework of self-care is somewhat akin to acquiring armour for yourself. Once you have the armour in place, you can use the pieces necessary as your adoption or foster situation warrants. A large piece of this armour comes from putting a strong support network in place ahead of time.

Ideally, this support network will consist of people from more than one area of your life such as family, friends, neighbours, co-workers, people from your church or organization, and even online acquaintances and friends. It is important for this network to originate from different sources because you will need more than one type of support. However it is that these people fit into your life, it is important to prepare them for what lies ahead and to let them know what you will need from them. Do not assume that just because you have been there to support them in the past, they will be there to support you. Also, don't assume that they will know how to support you without being asked. There will be people in your life who don't agree with or understand your decision to foster or adopt. If they choose not to be there for you, it is better to know this ahead of time. This is a reality for almost every foster and adoptive family that I know and there is a bit of grieving that needs to take place for that loss.

Prepare your support network. There are books and articles that are written for extended family and friends which you can reference in their entirety or you can draft your own letter to family and friends explaining to them what your intentions are and how you will need them. It's important in this letter to address what attachment will look like when your child first comes home. If you want to be the only one who is able to hold your child, people will be more prepared and less likely to be offended if it has been explained to them ahead of time and if they better understand the reason behind this decision. If you would like to have practical help after your child is home such as meals delivered, laundry done, or babysitting for your other kids, outline this in the letter. Most people want to help but may not know how best to help until it is explained to them.

There will be people in your support network who may be able to give you practical help through this journey such as babysitting to give you a break, picking up a few groceries so that you don't have to pack up the kids who all have colds, or helping you tidy up the house after a long day. Accept this help.

Then there will be people that you will need to be your emotional support who you can vent to, cry to, and maybe even scream at, and who will listen without judgment and still love you.

There will need to be people in your support network that you can just have fun with and ease the stress by helping you laugh, offering encouragement, and lifting you up.

There will also need to be people in your support network who "get it". The first three types of support you need will probably come from people already in your life, but this last type will be something you will need to create. Again, it's best if you can create this ahead of time.

There is nothing quite like being able to talk to someone who "gets it", someone who has been there and done that, and most importantly, someone who has survived to tell the tale! Seek out people who have also adopted or fostered. The internet is a great resource for this as you will be able to find others who are adopting children from the same country you are adopting from, fostering kids with the same types of special needs, adopting with a large family, have adopted trans-racially or many other types of similarities. If you are planning to homeschool, I run a Facebook group specifically for Homeschooling Adopted Children that you can request to join. The group's members are engaged, supportive and full of information.

Online support specific to parents who have high needs children can be found in The Chaos and The Clutter Community Center. It includes resources and encouragement, but most importantly, a way to find that magical "me too" moment.

Following someone's blog or meeting in a Facebook group can lead to emailing, phone calls and a true friendship being formed on the basis of shared interests and commonalities. This support will prove to be invaluable.

It is important, however, to also seek out relationships in real life that meet these characteristics. There are many fostering and adoption support groups. Find one that meets in your area and attend it even before you bring your child home. Begin to lay the groundwork for this support network in your life. It will become increasingly important later and it is also important for your child to meet other fostered or adopted children to create a normalcy around their story and to begin to form a future support network for them.

It has been a huge blessing in our life to be able to get together with other families formed by fostering and adoption. At times, our backyard is filled with families where most of the kids are adopted or fostered and it's nice for them to be in a situation where that is "normal". Our kids think that it's perfectly normal for white parents to be raising black children and that one of our closest friends is black and raising white and First Nations children. It's important for the kids to be able to play in that type of setting, but it's equally important for me to be able to sit around discussing hair care and attachment with other moms and to be able to share ideas and ask each other the hard questions.

I formed much of my own support network myself. I walked up to moms that appeared to me to be foster or adoptive moms in libraries, at homeschool events and at the playground and struck up conversations.

Some of those women are now among my closest friends and we have created an incredible support network for ourselves. We can talk openly about our struggles, ask each other for advice and be able to offer practical support to one another too such as meals or chauffeuring or child care when one of us is in the midst of a crisis.

Triage

Now that you have laid a solid foundation and are as fully prepared as you can be to welcome a child into your home, the real self-care begins.

When your new child first arrives home, life tends to become more like triage in an emergency room. Your attention goes to whatever is absolutely critical and everything else, including taking care of yourself, falls to the wayside. A child who is having tantrums, rages, and meltdowns naturally has a way of demanding your attention.

Internationally adopted children can have health issues, such as parasites and fungus, and can be suffering the effects of long-term malnutrition. This will mean a series of appointments, trips to the pharmacy, multiple stops at the lab, and of course, the lovely task of collecting a series of stool samples from children who may not speak your language and to whom you are basically a stranger. Add to the list all of the running around necessary to complete paperwork such as name changes, applying for health coverage, getting passport photos (and trying to explain to a child who speaks little English NOT to smile for the camera this time!), and standing in line to get the passport. It is little wonder that adoptive parents find themselves feeling like their needs have to take a backseat to those of their new addition!

The first days of a foster child placement in your home are just as hectic. You meet with the child's caseworker, take the child for a full medical exam, fill out the necessary forms, and attempt to catch yourself up on the child's history by contacting any professionals such as teachers, therapists, and doctors who have been involved with the child. This all has to take place while the child is trying to adjust to being uprooted, learn about your family and decipher their place in it.

People may assume that the adjustment to the adoption of a newborn would be easier when it comes to self-care, but that is a misperception. With a newborn, there are still the sleepless nights, the appointments, and paperwork. In cases of open adoption, some adoptive mothers feel added pressure to do everything perfectly because the birth mother chose them and is entrusting them to take care of the child. This can lead quickly to burnout.

When you feel as though you are only reacting to things, as opposed to being proactive, putting out fires that are directly in front of you, and cannot think two steps ahead, you are living in triage.

Triage is a dangerous place to live because there is no self-care happening at all. Though technically things that absolutely need to get done are getting done, no one in the family is able to have their needs fully met in this stage. This stage can easily lead to depression, burnout, marital breakdown, and health complications.

When you already feel as though you are not meeting the emotional needs of your children, it may go against everything logical in you to put yourself first. However, when you are in the triage stage, that is exactly what you need to do. I am not talking about being selfish. I am talking about helping yourself so that you can better help your family. I am talking about taking a breath. When you feel like you are drowning (which is what living in triage feels like) and the thought of taking a breath seems impossible, remember that it is necessary.

What does taking a breath look like? Taking a breath means stopping right now and literally taking a breath.

Step 1: Breathe in through your nose and out through your mouth. And again. And again.

Step 2: Now tell yourself that you cannot do it all right now and that is okay. Tell yourself that you need help. Tell yourself that this is only for a season and that you will get through it.

Step 3: Admit that you need help.

Step 4: Walk over to the phone. Yes, even if the kids are screaming in the background and one is clinging to your leg, still pick the phone up. Call the one person that you know will help you in a tangible, practical way.

Step 5: Ask for help. Be specific. It's okay to say, "I need you to come right now," or "I don't know what you can do to help, but can you please come and help me figure it out?"

Often when living in triage, you cannot even imagine what someone else could do, so even when people around you offer their help, you don't know what to ask for. This is the time to admit that you don't even know what they could do, but you need them to do something.

Step 6: Sit down with a pen and paper, perhaps along with the person you called, and start writing down things you need to do. Your list may have things on it like:

- Make supper
- Do laundry
- Change sheets
- Pick up groceries
- Make doctor appointments
- Call so-and-so
- Tidy the house
- Shower
- Comb hair
- Read child a story

When you see it on paper, you will realize that most of the list can be delegated. No one likes to ask for help or admit that they cannot do it all. This next step is hard. It has to be done.

Step 7: Delegate. If there is no one in your extended family or circle of friends that you can ask to help you with some of the items on your list, call a local church or community centre and ask if they can help, or have the person that you phoned make this call.

If you still cannot find help, hire help. Hire a housekeeper. Hire a mother's helper. Hire a service to pick up your groceries. The fact that I do not take the stress of debt or additional bills lightly and am suggesting that you do this should demonstrate how important it is!

This time of triage does not have to last long, but you will need help to get you through it. If you do not get help and begin to take care of yourself in this stage, it will be prolonged and may lead to things becoming even more critical.

Once you have established some practical help, you need to put yourself onto the triage list. Your new child is obviously your biggest priority at the moment, but it will be more beneficial to them if you have something to offer. You need to begin by taking care of yourself first.

Step 8: Shower every day. If you are reading this and living in triage, you may be thinking that this is impossible. It may mean getting up earlier, which may not seem possible when you are already so tired, jet lagged or getting up in the night with a baby. It may mean changing your routine to shower at night instead. It may mean bringing your child in the shower with you. Shower.

Step 9: Get dressed in real clothes, do your hair, and put some make-up on. By now, you probably think I have lost my mind! I am serious. You need to look good so that you feel good. Wearing sweatpants or pajamas might seem easier and more comfortable, but it takes the same amount of time to put on jeans or dress pants and will improve your mood and your energy level.

Step 10: Eat. I know that this seems like a given, but if you are living in triage or have in the past, you know that this can sometimes fall to the bottom of the list. Evening can come around and you may just realize that you have not yet eaten. You may spend time during the day ensuring that your kids eat and even cleaning up the dishes afterwards, but your meals are probably not regular and probably even less healthy. Make a decision that no matter what, you will eat. This may mean spending money on having groceries or meals delivered. This may mean having to ask your spouse to keep you accountable for eating.

The easiest way to ensure that you are eating healthy is to prepare some snack style foods for yourself the night before. Cut up some vegetables, fruit, and cheese. Having these things on hand, as well as some healthy muffins, crackers, and breads, will make it easier for you to eat when you can and to ensure that what is going into your body is as healthy as possible.

Step 11: Drink water. This sounds easy, but is another tricky thing to follow through on. When your body does not get enough water, you will be more fatigued and have a harder time thinking clearly. Make it a priority to always have a glass of water with you or beside you. Clip a water bottle to your belt loop if you have to.

Step 12: Go easy on yourself and your spouse. This time will not last forever. Give yourself permission to get through it without doing everything perfectly. Allow yourself grace and give the same to your spouse. Communication with your partner will likely be at a minimum during this time since so much of your energy is expended elsewhere, so communicate the fact that you are in this together and will make it through.

By following these 12 steps, you will be able to carry yourself through the time of triage and get to a point where things are less overwhelming. You will get to the other side.

Perfectionism and PADS

One of the biggest traps that we fall into, especially as women, is the trap of perfectionism. (my apologies to the handful of men reading this book!) We put expectations on ourselves that no human being would ever be able to live up to and then we beat ourselves up when we fall short of those expectations. We also expect that our bonding with our new child will be instant.

Once your adopted or foster child is home, there have been months or even years of anticipation built up. You have imagined what your life would be like once your child came home and imagined the type of mother you would be. When you begin to feel overwhelmed, you may be afraid to ask for help out of worry about what others will think. You may be afraid that people will feel this is what you deserve because you are the one who wanted to adopt or foster and are worried about them judging you. This only compounds your feelings of isolation.

If during the time of triage you do not ask for help and fail to recognize the seriousness of your feelings, depression can set in. Post Adoption Depression Syndrome (PADS) is very real. The rates for PADS are as high as the rates for Postpartum Depression (PPD). PADS is not something that is spoken about often and the symptoms are easily missed by friends, family members, doctors, and social workers, which compounds the issue with a lack of information, support, and access to help. The symptoms of PADS are:

Diagnostic Criteria From DSM-IV

- Feeling sad, empty, or depressed most of the day, every day
- Irritability
- Diminished interest or pleasure in all or most activities

- Significant weight loss or gain
- Increase or decrease in appetite
- Insomnia (having trouble sleeping) or hypersomnia (wanting to sleep more)
- Fatigue
- Loss of energy
- Restlessness
- Feelings of worthlessness nearly every day
- Feelings of guilt nearly every day
- "Diminished" ability to think or concentrate nearly every day
- Indecisiveness
- Difficulty with memory
- Suicidal thoughts or ideation

If you recognize several of these symptoms in yourself or your spouse and they persist for more than two weeks, it is important that you seek outside help immediately. Call your doctor, adoption social worker, or mental health professional to get support systems in place.

There are support groups for PADS and PPD that can be extremely helpful in offering hope for those who are suffering from the symptoms. Your doctor may prescribe anti-depressant medication and suggest counselling.

PADS is most common among mothers who adopt older children and in first time mothers, but can also strike new fathers, veteran adoptive mothers, and adoptive mothers of newborns.

The most important thing to remember if you are suffering from PADS is that you are not alone. Seek out the help of a professional and follow their advice. Recovery will happen.

♥♥ Secondary Trauma ♥♥

Secondary trauma, also sometimes referred to as vicarious trauma, can affect therapists, first responders and primary caregivers. By bearing witness to the trauma of others, you can take some of that trauma on for yourself.

The DSM states that trauma can affect those who survive a traumatic event, those who witness a traumatic event or those who hear of a traumatic event that affected someone of significance to them. It then stands to reason that parents who hear of their adopted child's past trauma would be at risk of developing secondary trauma.

Some of the signs of secondary trauma include:

- having difficulty talking about your feelings
- feeling diminished joy towards things you once enjoyed
- feeling trapped
- having a limited range of emotion but anger and irritation always
- being present
- having an exaggerated startle response
- intrusive thoughts of your child's history
- nightmares
- feelings of hopelessness
- trouble sleeping
- worrying
- exhaustion
- apathy
- problems with intimacy
- feeling withdrawn and isolated
- feeling impatient
- questioning your worldview
- feeling detached
- low self-image

-perfectionism

There are some strategies that can help combat symptoms of secondary trauma. Exercise that increases your heart rate for at least 12 minutes a day, five days a week, can decrease symptoms. Focusing on your breathing and using mindfulness have also been shown to help. For mindfulness, you can use yoga, a mindfulness app on your phone, gratitude, prayer, or meditation. Finding a support group of others who have walked a similar road can be therapeutic. Individual or family counseling may also be helpful.

For myself, I find that yoga is helpful once I am actually in the class, but rarely make the time for it. I regularly use a combination of prayer and purposeful gratitude.

Hearing about your child's past trauma can trigger your own trauma history which is also something to be aware of. If you find that your symptoms are worsening or significantly interfering with your life, seek the help of a licensed therapist.

One further note regarding trauma: secondary trauma can occur from hearing about your child's past trauma but, as a foster or adoptive parent, you can also be at risk of developing full PTSD (Post Traumatic Stress Disorder). This can happen as a result of your child's behaviors, for instance if you are attacked or placed at risk. PTSD can also occur if your spouse or other children are harmed or if behaviours occur that require legal intervention. If you suspect you may be suffering from PTSD, seek help from a medical professional or licensed therapist.

 Loss

In adoption and foster care, there is much loss for the children who are being placed in a new home, but there can also be loss for the parent. Foster parents often have to say goodbye to children in their care when they are moved back to the birth family, to another placement, or to an adoptive home. Sometimes there is relief in this in the case of a difficult placement, but most often, there is tremendous sadness and grief.

Adoptive parents also face loss. The first parent may change their mind and decide to parent the baby, leaving the adoptive parents with empty hearts and an empty crib. The country they are adopting from may suddenly shut down or change their regulations, making an adoption from there impossible, perhaps marking the death of a dream for that family. In times like these, self-care is critical. It is also important to acknowledge the enormity of the loss and to allow time and space for grieving.

There are other kinds of loss in adoption and fostering as well. The loss of your independence, the loss of family or friends who don't support your decision, the loss perhaps of the dream of having biological children, the loss of your family as you knew it, the loss of your alone time…these are very real. Give yourself permission to grieve in the way that you need to.

Shortly after we began fostering, we were asked about the possibility of taking a baby at birth with a very high likelihood (98%) of being able to adopt the baby in the future. We excitedly agreed and when we brought our daughter Amera home at just three days old, we never considered that we would be the family that fell into that other 2%. We loved her with abandon, holding nothing back, and when we lost her 20 months later, we were stunned and heartbroken. The daughter of our hearts would never be our daughter on paper.

In the days that followed, it was our support system and faith in God that got us through. The words that were carefully written in cards that I keep to this day encouraged me and let me know that I was not alone in my anguish. A few friends dropped off casseroles and snacks. One friend drove from three hours away just to sit with me. Another friend phoned me almost daily to tell me what activity she and I were going to do that day.

Since it was summer and I was in too much of a daze to argue with her, it got me and the other kids out of the house and helped me to learn to live again. Having to care for another foster baby that we also intended to adopt (who is now our forever daughter, Gracelyn), forced me to get out of bed every morning. Our friends and family grieved for Amera, too. At the time, it felt like the pain would never end, but we found a way to go on and selfcare, our faith, and our friends and family all made it possible to move forward and to even find happiness again.

Marriage ❤❤

One of the issues that is rarely spoken of in the adoptive community is the effect adoption can have on marriages. Though the actual statistics seem illusive at best, divorce rates among adoptive parents are reported to be higher than that of the general population. Parenting children with special needs and infertility are also two factors that increase divorce rates and those are present in many adoptive homes. While that is not good news for adoptive parents, there are things that can be done to help protect your marriage.

Some of the things that can place a strain on even the strongest of marriages for adoptive families include:

Public Scrutiny – Parents face a lot of scrutiny, from friends, family, strangers at the store, schools, medical professionals and more. It's a part of parenting, but for adoptive parents, the scrutiny goes to a much more invasive and deeper level . Adoptive parents are scrutinized for everything from what type of adoption they chose to pursue, to their choice to bottle or breastfeed, to their discipline methods, to their stand on immunizations, to their decision to change or keep their child's first given name, to the way in which they choose to incorporate their child's culture, to their decision to be or not be a multi-racial family, to their methods of attachment, to the foods they feed their children and more. Add to that the pressure to be the best parent possible because a birth mother is entrusting you to raise the most precious thing imaginable or an entire country has allowed you to take one of their most important natural resources and that's a pretty weighty thing! And then of course there is that most intrusive scrutiny of all – the home study. This is where a complete stranger comes into your home and because they have the title of Social Worker, they are allowed to ask you all kinds of intimate details and give their opinions of your parenting (even if they are 19 years old and have no children or nieces or nephews, but I digress!) and they ask about your sex life and about your childhood and about the whys of all the decisions you've made. I am not saying that checks and balances should not be put in place. I am merely pointing out that all this public scrutiny and pressure can put a strain on a relationship over time.

Sleep Deprivation – This is not unique to adoptive families, but can be exaggerated by things such as time change/jet lag in the case of international adoption, drug or alcohol exposure of a baby prenatally, and that adoptive families tend to have larger families, making their years of sleep deprivation longer. Lack of sleep can change your perspective on many things. If you're too tired at the end of the day, you don't take the time to talk or perhaps to do other 'bedroom activities' that may be critical for a healthy marriage.

Special Needs – Adoption increases the chances that you will have a child with special needs. Among the most obvious special needs of adopted children are those related to prenatal exposures such as FASD (fetal alcohol spectrum disorder) and Fetal Drug Effect. Other special needs that are more common in adopted children than in the general population include Reactive Attachment Disorder, Sensory Processing Disorder, Attention Deficit Disorder, and Developmental Trauma Disorder or Post Traumatic Stress Disorder.

Infertility – Many come to adoption after years of infertility. The stress of that and the strain that puts on a relationship, on a sex life, and on finances, is high. Some infertility treatments cause mood swings for the wife, which can be pretty unpleasant in a marriage too. So now these couples who have already suffered so much hurt and loss and grief embark on another road of ups and downs where the outcome is not always clear and the scars of the years of infertility are still there. The hurts are often still raw and, for some, that pain never goes away. For others, they come to the realization that adoption wasn't meant to be Plan B but was God's plan A for their family all along.

Financial Strain – The number one cause of divorce in Canada and the United States is conflict over finances. Infertility treatments are very expensive and some couples have already wiped out all their savings on that before they even get to adoption. Domestic open adoption, private adoption, and international adoption are all very expensive. Adopting through local foster care is often free.

Disparity – In almost all cases of adoption, one spouse wants it more than the other. Sometimes, they both really want it, but often one is the driving force while the other is going along with it to make their spouse happy. That can obviously cause tremendous strain later on if there are problems adjusting. This type of disparity gives room for a lot of resentment to build.

Conflict – In any marriage, there are so many potential areas for conflict but the ones added by adoption may include things like disagreeing on birth family contact, discipline in regards to challenging behaviors, how to work on attachment, how to deal with questions in public, what to tell your children regarding their history, and adopting future children. There is a lot of talk in the adoption world about preparing yourself for attachment issues and toddler tantrums and parasites but preparing your marriage is rarely mentioned. I encourage those who are still waiting to adopt to add some marriage books to their reading list in addition to those books about adoption and attachment. "Love and Respect" and "The Five Love Languages" are a good place to start.

The first year home with your child may be difficult on your marriage. As a couple, you will have far less time for each other and your relationship will undergo some major changes. As a family, there is a lot of adjustments to be made, so if at all possible, just get through that first year any way you can and don't make any life-changing decisions until after that first year.

I am by no means an expert on marriage. There were years

where my husband and I barely managed to stay together, but we held on and have now been married for 21 years. When we were at our lowest point, marriage counselling helped, as did changing our communication styles, but what we found to be the most effective prescription for our marriage was instituting a weekly date night. I have suggested it to other couples who have seen it turn their marriages around as well. We have a set night each week that is our date night regardless of circumstances. If we can't find a babysitter, we have an at-home date night. If we don't have much money, we do something that's free. Putting in that time commitment and being able to be a couple once a week instead of just parents was the magic for us.

Protect your marriage by:
- working on your communication,
- putting in place weekly or at least monthly date nights,
- budget, attend marriage counselling or marriage retreats or seminars,
- take care of your own self-care and encourage your spouse to do the same.

Ongoing Self-Care

Once a family has gone through their initial time of transition with their new child, it is time to begin thinking about self-care in another way.

Adoptive and foster families have unique challenges and the general level of stress within them will continue to be higher than for an average family. For this reason, it is important that parents develop the habit of practicing ongoing self-care.

Humour

Especially if you are parenting a child with special needs, humour will be an effective tool for you to combat stress, protect your marriage, and elevate the level of joy in your home. For some, humour comes naturally. For those not in that category, infuse humour into your life. Watch funny movies, read comics, or go to see comedians perform. Teach your kids some clean jokes. Take a picture of the things your kids do that may not be funny now, but will probably be funny later (like when my son covered himself in Zincofax or when another one of my sons shaved off his eyebrows)! Taking a picture will instantly diffuse your anger and change your perspective. When your autistic son is repeating the same phrase for the millionth time that week, you can choose frustration and anger or you can choose humour. When you are taking your daughter to the hospital for the fifth time in three weeks, you can feel hopeless, or you can joke that they should start giving you frequent user perks like your own parking space. It's all in the attitude and the perspective! Those are things that you can control. Practice laughing for no reason. It's good for the stomach muscles, too.

Exercise

Incorporate exercise into your life. If you love to exercise, train for a half marathon, join a martial arts club, start a ball hockey team, or take a fitness class. If you are less enthusiastic about exercising, go out walking, do a workout DVD a few mornings a week, or dance around your kitchen with the kids. Exercising has a host of health benefits and can improve insomnia and lower stress. Exercising for just 10 minutes releases endorphins which improve your mood.

Truthfully, I hate exercising, but I force myself because I see what a difference it makes in my mood, my energy level and my ability to handle stress. I have an app on my phone that walks me through a 7 minute exercise regime every day. When the weather cooperates, I sometimes go for a walk with my neighbour which allows me to also get time to talk to another adult and to laugh. On days when the mood in the house needs changing, I put music on and dance in the kitchen with the kids which is good for all of us.

Relax

Do what relaxes you. Put it into your schedule (in permanent pen) and commit to it. This may be yoga, meditation, prayer, reading, going for a long walk, watching some mindless television, or taking a warm bath. Drink tea on your back deck while the sun sets. Give yourself a pedicure or make an appointment to have one done. Wake up before the kids and sit in a quiet room reflecting on the things for which you are grateful.

Journal

Journaling releases frustrations and is a wonderful creative outlet. Journaling when you are parenting foster or adoptive children has another benefit as well. Often, when you are in the midst of it, it is difficult to see progress from day to day. Journaling allows you to look back and track progress. When you read prior entries, you are able to see improvements in your child's attachment, behavior or development that you may miss when the changes happen so gradually. Some prefer blogging to journaling. The only caution with blogging is that for foster parents especially there can be legal implications for breach of privacy and venting online can have lasting consequences. A private journal in addition to blogging is an easy fix for this problem.

Bedtimes

Put your kids to bed early to ensure they are getting enough sleep. In turn, they will be less grumpy during the days, learn more easily, retain that knowledge, and be better able to fight off infections. Those are good things that will indirectly help with your self-care. Putting your kids to bed earlier will also help your self-care directly by giving you time to decompress in the evenings. You need time to unwind and be out of parenting mode. Allowing yourself this break every day will ensure that you are better able to handle whatever the next day holds and you have the time to fit self-care into your life. Creating a routine that includes early bedtimes is also important for your relationship with your spouse. You need time together. You need to protect that time.

Sleep

Get enough sleep. If you are not getting enough sleep at night because of kids waking you or insomnia, find a way to take a short nap at least twice a week. Your body and your brain need sleep.

Counselling

Therapy for yourself and/or your kids can be a preventative measure. You do not need to wait until there is a crisis before seeking out professional help. Not everyone is comfortable using the services of a counsellor, but it should certainly be an option to consider when the stress begins to pile up or there are issues and behaviours in your children that you do not know how to handle. Admitting that you need help is a good thing. A good counsellor will also be able to give you ideas to promote attachment, manage behaviours, and improve communication in your home.

Hobbies

Find a hobby that brings you joy. Consider photography, cooking, bird watching, snow shoeing, scrapbooking, blogging, writing, painting, playing an instrument, collecting, gardening, knitting, antiquing, sewing, pottery, quilting, golfing, or woodworking.

Hobbies can create an opportunity to make something lasting, which is a great contrast to the clean laundry that gets dirty again, the freshly mopped floors that get messy again, and the food you slaved over that quickly gets eaten. Creating something lasting such as a scrapbook page, scarf, vase, or story leaves a feeling of accomplishment and pride. Hobbies are also a creative outlet and can be a healthy release of stress. Having something in your life other than parenting and working is important. Find a hobby that you enjoy.

Set the Alarm

Setting the alarm so that you wake up even 20 minutes before your kids do allows you to start the day off peacefully and on your own terms. Use this time to do what will energize you and best prepare you for the day. For some, this will be exercise or getting fresh air. For others, this will be having time alone with God in devotion and prayer. For others, this will be having a cup of coffee or tea in silence and just breathing.

Give Yourself a Break

Parenting is hard. Foster and adoptive parenting is harder. Parenting a child with special needs is even that much harder. You need to remind yourself of this and cut yourself some slack. It is okay to not be perfect. Lower the expectations you have of yourself.

Recharge

Everyone needs a break once in awhile. Recharge your batteries by getting away. Taking a parenting, attachment, fostering, or adoption seminar or conference can give you much-needed time away from the responsibilities at home while at the same time giving you additional coping skills and tools for managing things upon your return. A day or weekend like this is worth the time, money, and scheduling difficulties it takes to plan. However, there will come times when you need to shut off your parenting brain. In those times, a night or weekend away at a woman's retreat, scrapbooking retreat, or friend or relative's house is probably just what is needed to refuel your tank and renew your energy.

I know that I wrote that flippantly as if getting child care is easy. As the mom of 7 kids, 5 of whom have special needs, I know that it isn't. I know that this is not something that is possible for everyone. You may not have friends or family that can help. You may be a single parent who doesn't have a spouse to leave the kids with for a weekend getaway with friends. I wrote it that way because I believe it to be such a priority that I'm hoping you will try to think outside the box to find a way. Is there a parent in your support network you could exchange kids with so that you could get a break one weekend and they could get a break another? Is there a family or young couple at your church that could be trusted to come stay in your home while you and your spouse go away for just one night? Could you set money aside every month so that once a year you could hire a sitter to come in so that you and your spouse could get time away together?

Pockets of Time

Time is something that is impossible to increase. You can, however, be in control of what you do with your time. Even in the chaos of a busy life, there are moments that you can grab ahold of and make the best of them.

Time in the car is a great example of this. For working parents especially, this time of the day may be their only chance to have time for themselves.

Use the time in your vehicle to promote your self-care by praying aloud, listening to music that you love while singing at the top of your lungs, or turning off the music and relishing in the silence. If there is a motivational speaker or author that encourages you, purchase those books on CD or download podcasts on your iPod and listen to them as you drive.

If there is never a time when you are alone in your vehicle, teach your kids The Quiet Game. The Quiet Game is when everyone is completely quiet and the one who is quiet the longest gets a prize or bragging rights. Be sure to encourage those kids who have a more difficult time with this by giving them praise as they go so that they will still want to play even if they rarely win.

There are many other opportunities to create tiny pockets of time that you can make the best of such as sitting in a waiting room (I always carry a book in my purse just in case), the rare morning when the kids sleep in, or the time after supper as you are doing the dishes while the kids make one last dash to the backyard to play.

Environment

Surround yourself with things that make you smile. Your home should be an oasis for you. By ridding it of clutter (though I am still working on that one myself) and by bringing in things that bring you a feeling of peace or joy, you will create a sanctuary for yourself. Play music that you like. Set out flowers if they remind you of the beauty in the world. Your children will also respond well to a more pleasant environment. This also applies to people. Surround yourself with positive people who bring out the best in you.

Spiritual Health

Nurturing yourself spiritually is as important, if not more important, than nurturing yourself physically and emotionally. This will look different for different people depending on their spiritual beliefs, but there are some common things that can help you to get the most out of your spiritual life. These include prayer or meditation, having belief, faith, and hope, worshipping or listening to uplifting music, and surrounding yourself with a community of people who share your beliefs and can encourage you on your spiritual path. It is also freeing to give God control of that which you cannot control.

Acceptance

As with many situations in life, fostering and adoption may have brought about things which you were not expecting or prepared for. These may include things such as parenting a child with special needs that you were unaware of before placement, loss of friends who do not agree with your choices, or changes in your routine, marriage or home. It is important that you are able to distinguish which things in your life you can change and which you cannot. Identifying these will help you regain a sense of control. Once these have been identified, it may be helpful to memorize the Serenity Prayer: "Lord, grant me the serenity to accept the things I cannot change, the courage to change the things I can, and the wisdom to know the difference." As some of the changes in your life could potentially lead to resentment, learning to accept the things that you cannot change will ultimately relieve the frustration and begin to lessen the resentment.

Socialize

Certain circumstances in foster and adoptive families such as having a large family, parenting children who have public outbursts or difficult behaviour, or managing children with special needs may limit your ability to socialize. However, it is still important to find ways to create a social life and to make it a priority to have human contact with other adults. You can do this by inviting over another family like yours, getting together at a playground with another mom and her kids for a play date, or going to a mom's morning out group that offers childcare. One way we have found that allows us to maintain a small but real social life is to have another couple over for dinner after our kids are in bed. By feeding the kids first and tucking them in, we can entertain without interruptions. If the other couple has difficulty getting childcare, we plan an evening where we feed all the kids first (theirs and ours) and then try to settle the kids in to an activity or watching a movie while we eat our dinner. It's not perfect, but it works!

The other thing that has helped our social life tremendously is having friends who are also foster or adoptive parents and also have children with special needs. This means that we can get together with them without feeling that our parenting or our children's behaviour is being judged. We get together as families and play board games or the adults visit while the kids run around the yard.

Take Breaks

Taking regular breaks is an important element for ongoing self-care. Arrange for regular time outs for yourself to recharge. If you have friends or family members who can help with child care, that is ideal. For many, accessing child care may be difficult. There may be programs available in your state or province that offer cost relief on respite care or babysitting, particularly if you have special needs children. Some will even cover the cost of a housekeeper once a month. If you are still unable to find child care even after contacting services in your community, have your spouse or a friend watch the kids for an hour while you go for a walk or take a bubble bath. Taking time for yourself is necessary. Having it set up as a regularly scheduled event will help you to get through the hard days knowing that a break is on the horizon.

When we were foster parents, we were offered respite care, a program where your foster children are cared for in another foster home for a day, a weekend or even a week to either give your family a break or to allow for vacations in cases where the child is not allowed out of the province. For many years, we refused respite care, not wanting our foster kids to feel like they weren't a part of our family, but in retrospect, that was a mistake. We should have taken advantage of the opportunity to fill our tanks and therefore, be able to have more patience and energy with the kids and each other. Eventually, we did accept occasional respite care and our only regret was not having done it sooner.

Expectations

The key to managing expectations is to keep your expectations for your child realistic without putting limits on the child. My husband and I maintain that our job as parents is to provide the opportunity for each of our children to reach their fullest possible potential. This may be for them to become a spouse, parent, and world renowned brain surgeon or it may be for them to be able to successfully live semi-independently while maintaining a positive attitude and a compassion for others. It is important that you not limit your children by their disabilities or challenges, but that you give them the freedom to achieve whatever successes and accomplishments they can in life.

It is equally important that you do not have unrealistic expectations. If you expect your children to attain goals that are clearly not possible given their circumstances, you will be setting yourself up for disappointment. It is also imperative that you keep these same things in mind for your parenting. You cannot expect too much of yourself. You are human, though often being the parent of a traumatized child or a child with special needs calls you to be superhuman!

Small Joys

Find small things that bring you joy and really hold onto those. Similar to the idea of practising gratitude, focusing on the small joys in your life will help you when times are hard. For myself, our once a month supper club gives me something to look forward to, walks with my neighbour Christie can always be counted on to bring me a smile and being in the practise of finding five things every day that I am thankful for no matter how small all help me to find joy even in the midst of difficult circumstances.

Celebrate

Celebrate the small victories. It is the baby steps and the tiny accomplishments that lead towards the bigger goals. Celebrate it all. Cherish the gifts that your child possesses instead of focusing on the challenges and remind yourself often of how far they (and you) have come.

♥♥ My Story - How I Got Here ♥♥

This book came about largely as a result of my own failings when it came to self-care. During our years as foster parents, I took far too long to accept help or book respite. I suffered, which meant that my kids suffered because they had a mom who was frazzled and tired. As an adoptive mom, I also allowed pride and independence to get in the way of healthier choices such as admitting that I couldn't do it all. Years of putting myself last and running kids to their appointments and therapies took a toll on my marriage, my health, my friendships, and my mental well-being. I don't want others to make the same mistakes I made.

Parenting children with a history of trauma led to me developing secondary trauma. Their behaviours and reactions as a result of their prior trauma caused me to develop PTSD (Post Traumatic Stress Disorder). My PTSD impacted my ability to parent effectively, particularly when it came to my two kids who have PTSD themselves, as well as Reactive Attachment Disorder. I was able to find healing for most of my symptoms by going to a professional therapist and, particularly, by going for EMDR therapy. I had researched its effectiveness with sufferers of PTSD, but was amazed at the difference it made for me. If you suspect that you have secondary trauma or PTSD, I highly recommend you find a licensed therapist who is trained in EMDR.

Self-care is still not something that comes naturally for me. It has been a process. Like anything, the more I do, the easier it becomes. Going for brisk walks with my neighbour or with my husband has been particularly effective because it combines fresh air, exercise and talking to another adult. When I begin to let my self-care slide, I can see a difference in my patience, my ability to cope with stress, and my energy level. As I continue on this journey towards getting healthier myself, so that I can better provide for the needs of my kids, I hope that I can inspire you to embark on the journey yourself. Your family will be healthier for it.

❤❤ Self-Care Ideas for Moms ❤❤

- Drink hot tea or coffee in a mug that brings you joy.

- Dance in your kitchen.

- Colour.

- Go for a walk with a friend.

- Sing (loudly) in the car or shower.

- Call a friend.

- Light some scented candles.

- Give yourself a pedicure. Choose a fun polish colour.

- Literally put yourself on the calendar.

- Watch a favourite or feel-good movie.

- Breathe deeply.

- Read before bed.

- Cuddle up under a blanket.

- Take a yoga or Pilates class.

- Go to church.

- Join a book club.

- Journal.

- Buy yourself a treat like flowers or chocolate.

- Spend some time in nature.

- Be creative: cook, bake, paint, sketch, scrapbook.

- Spread Kindness to someone else.

- Have a picnic outside or in your living room.

- Join a support group either online or in your community.

- Go to bed early or sleep in.

- Take a long shower.

- Set a timer for ten minutes and declutter.

- Make yourself a doctor or dentist appointment and go.

- Go for dinner with friends.

- Attend couselling for yourself.

- Go for a drive alone.

- Smile at yourself in the mirror.

- Put up Post-its with inspirational quotes or scriptures.

- Take a long Epsom salts bath with dimmed lights.

- Keep a gratitude journal.

- Listen to music.

- Watch a funny video.

- Pray.

- Plant something.

- Wear something you love.

- Watch the sunset or sunrise.

❤❤ *Acknowledgements* ❤❤

As you can probably imagine, writing even a relatively short book is not something that a homeschooling mother of seven can pull off alone! First and foremost, to God, who has blessed me with my seven precious children and is the Author of my story, the Giver of my strength. To Mandi, who lovingly cared for my kids while I hid in the office or my closet to write, who brought me tea and made sure that I was eating. To my mom, who always encouraged and supported me and has helped in countless ways over the years. To Glenda, who is an inspiration and has become my sister, my second mother, my mentor. Glenda has been a foster parent for over thirty years and continues to love and serve hurting children in the most selfless way.

To Cathy, Deborah, Tyler, Carla, and Denise for reading my first draft and offering their advice and opinions. To the online adoption community, who have been a wonderful resource, support, and source of friendship over the years. I appreciate each of you more than you know.

To my tribe of fellow adoptive mommas who are my sanity and my support. I don't know how I would survive this without you all. Michelle, Rachel, Darci, Denise, Shannon, Lindsay, Shelley, the inspiring ladies in my Adoption War Room prayer group who are all adoptive mommas and who "get it".

To my husband Mark, my amazing kids, Mackenzie, Jonah, Gracelyn, Josiah, Elijah, Eliana, and Sedaya who are the best gifts in my life.

About the Author

Sharla Kostelyk is the mother of seven children, two through the miracle of birth and five through the miracle of adoption. She is far from the perfect parent but has a knack for getting back up after her failures. You can find her blogging about sensory, high needs parenting, and adoption at *The Chaos and The Clutter*. Sharla is passionate about helping other foster and adoptive families thrive. She has created a community of support for high needs parents known as *The Chaos and The Clutter Community Center*.

Made in United States
North Haven, CT
15 March 2022

17184940R00031